EASY PIANO HYMNS

FOR BEGINNERS

A BOOK OF MUSIC FOR PRAISE AND WORSHIP

COLLECTED AND ARRANGED BY
ANGELA MARSHALL

Easy Piano Hymns for Beginners

A Book of Music for Praise and Worship

ISBN: 9798838633774

Published by Avanell Publishing Inc

www.avanellpublishing.com

Bonus Downloads

This book includes free digital content.
Visit **www.avanellpublishing.com** or scan the QR code below
to access your bonus materials,

- Fully orchestrated recordings of each song

- Printable reference charts to use while you play

- Lessons and charts for left hand playing

- Practice tips to help you build your skills

- Sheet music of additional songs

Table of Contents

Table of Contents

How to Read Piano Music

A B C D E F G

Piano keys are named after the letters of the alphabet, but they only go to G!

The piano has black and white keys.
The black keys are arranged in groups of 2 and 3.

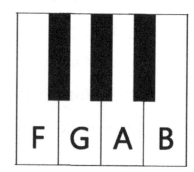

The letters **C D E**
are by a group of 2.

The letters **F G A B**
are by a group of 3.

The pattern of 2 and 3 repeats across the keyboard.
Use the groups of black keys to find the right notes on the piano.

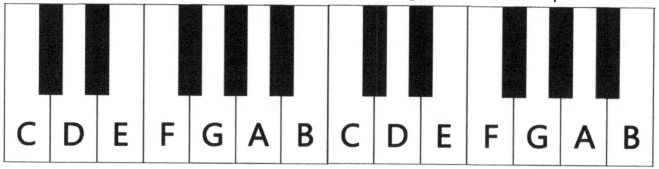

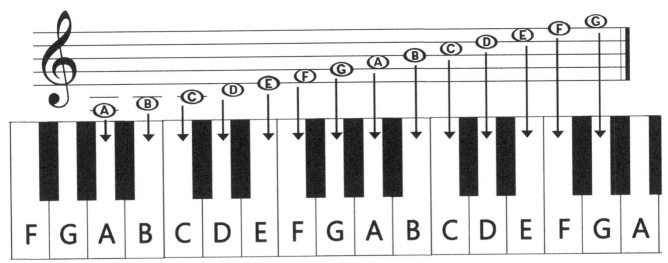

Each note is a letter of the musical alphabet and a key on the piano.

Each finger has a number.
Thumbs are number one!

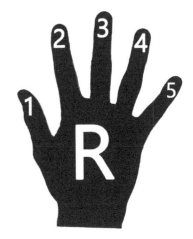

Each type of note gets a different number of beats.

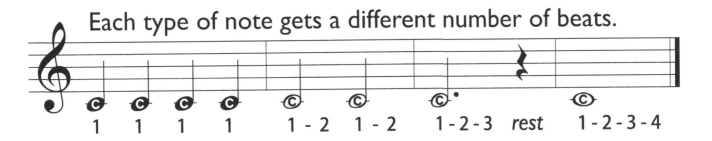

Level One

The songs in Level One only use five notes.

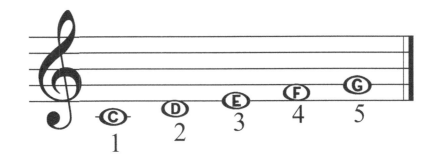

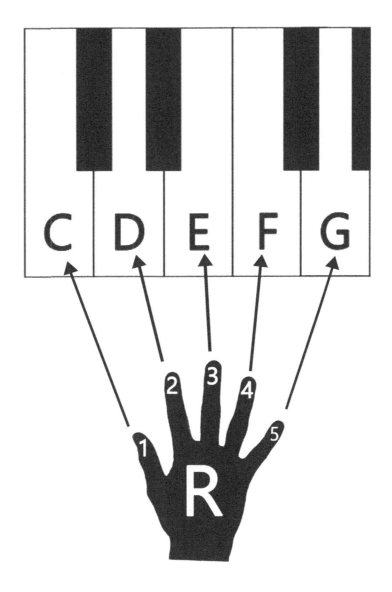

Hallelujah Chorus

George Frideric Handel

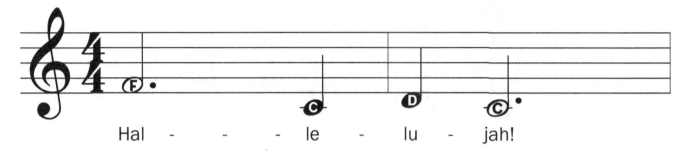

Hal - - - le - lu - jah!

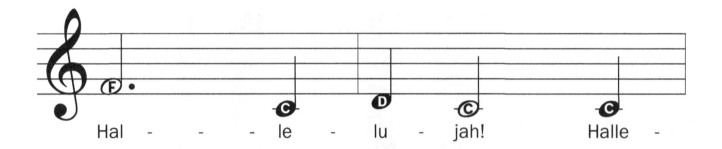

Hal - - - le - lu - jah! Halle -

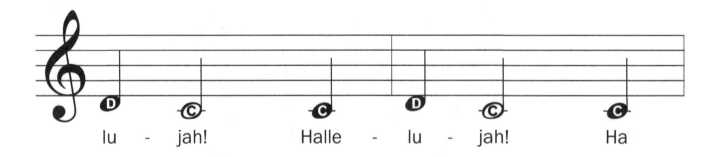

lu - jah! Halle - lu - jah! Ha

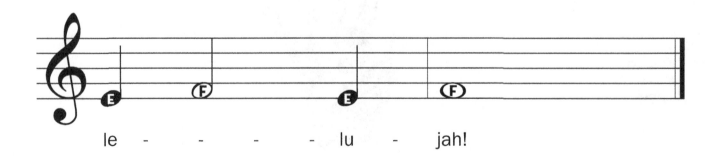

le - - - - - lu - jah!

God is So Good

Traditional

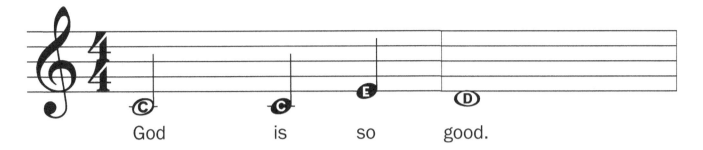

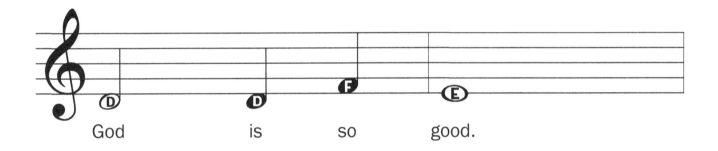

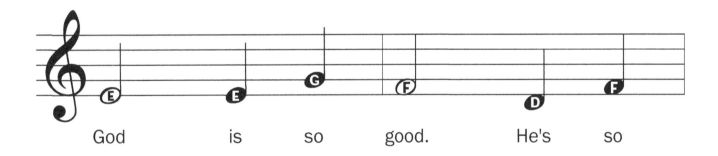

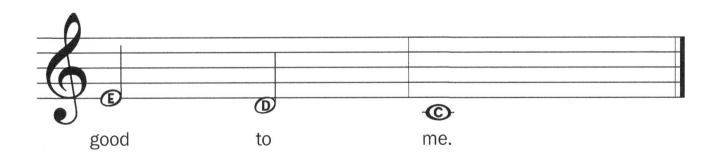

Shall We Gather at the River?

Robert Lowry

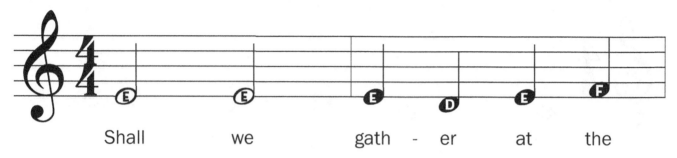

Shall   we   gath - er   at   the

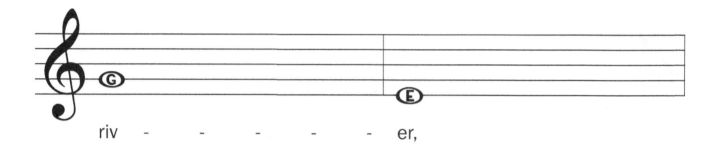

riv - - - - - er,

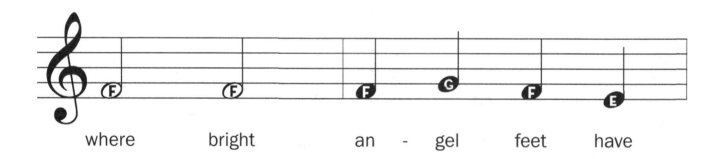

where   bright   an - gel   feet   have

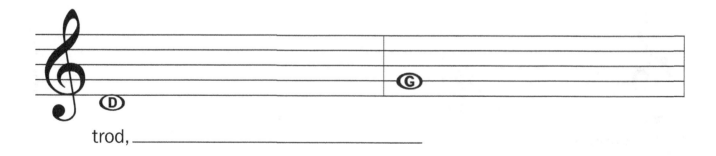

trod,_____

Shall We Gather at the River?

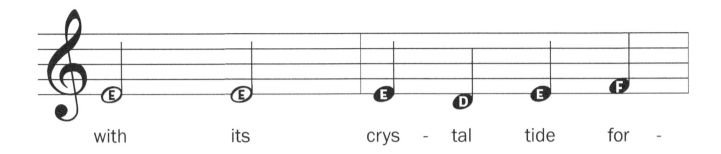

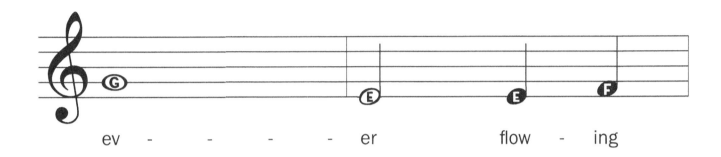

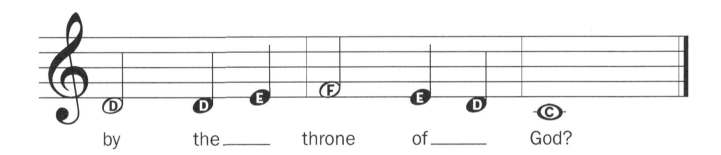

When the Saints Go Marching In

African American Spiritual

Oh, when the saints!

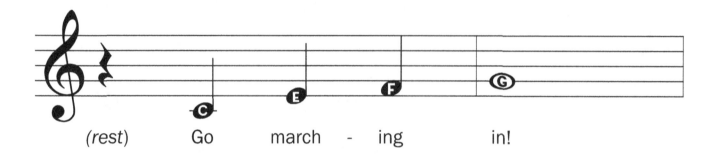

(rest) Go march - ing in!

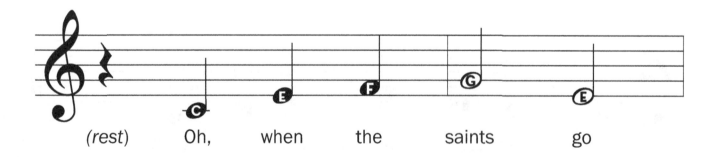

(rest) Oh, when the saints go

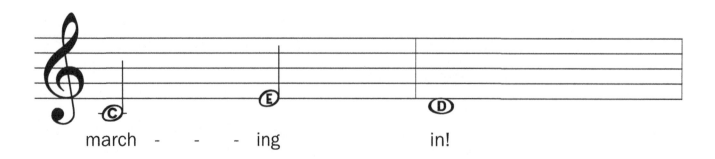

march - - - ing in!

When the Saints Go Marching In

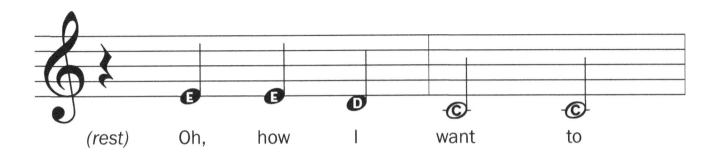

(rest)   Oh,   how   I   want   to

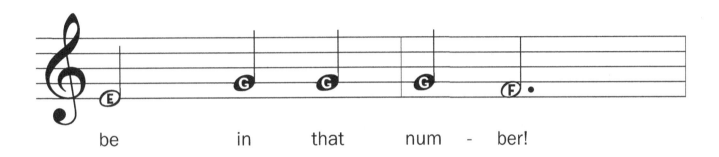

be   in   that   num - ber!

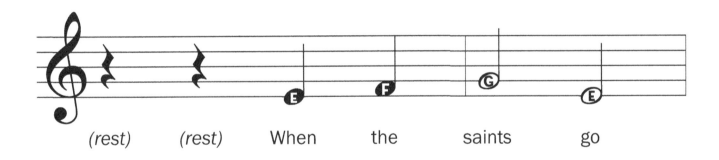

(rest)   (rest)   When   the   saints   go

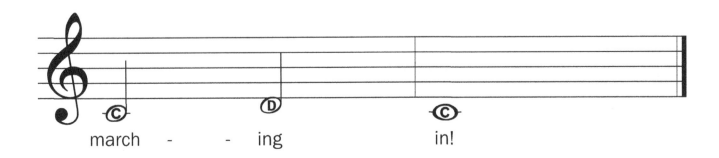

march - - ing   in!

Joyful, Joyful, We Adore Thee

Ludwig van Beethoven and Henry van Dyke

Joy - ful, joy - ful, we a - dore Thee,

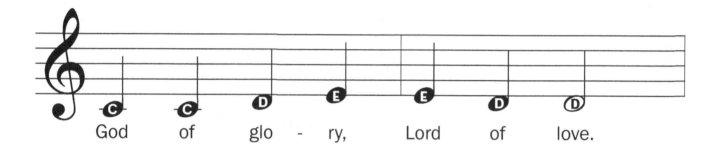

God of glo - ry, Lord of love.

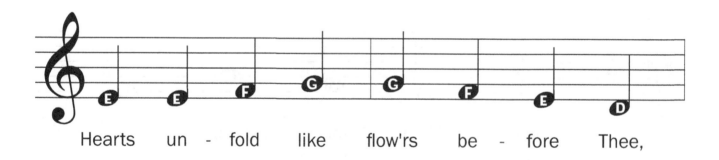

Hearts un - fold like flow'rs be - fore Thee,

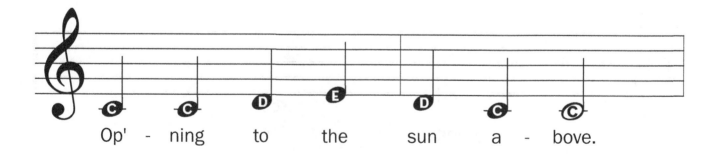

Op' - ning to the sun a - bove.

Joyful, Joyful, We Adore Thee

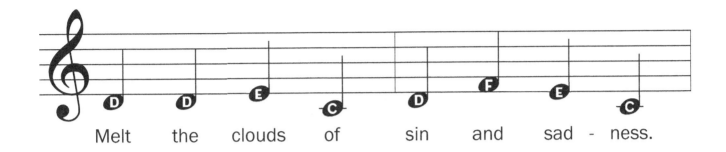

Melt   the   clouds   of   sin   and   sad - ness.

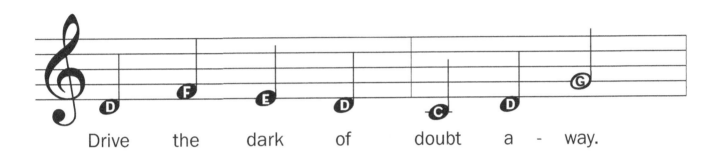

Drive   the   dark   of   doubt   a - way.

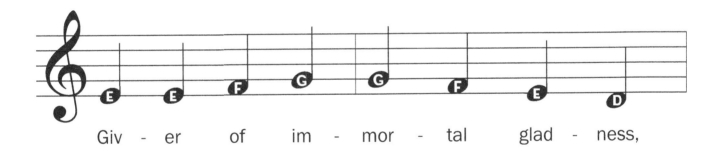

Giv - er   of   im - mor - tal   glad - ness,

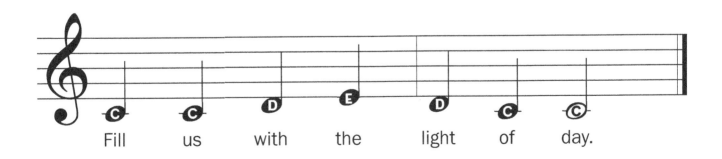

Fill   us   with   the   light   of   day.

Nothing but the Blood of Jesus

Robert Lowry

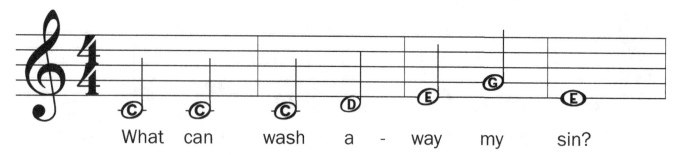

What can wash a - way my sin?

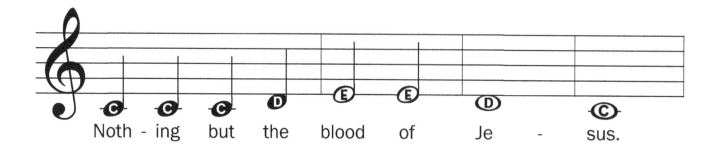

Noth - ing but the blood of Je - sus.

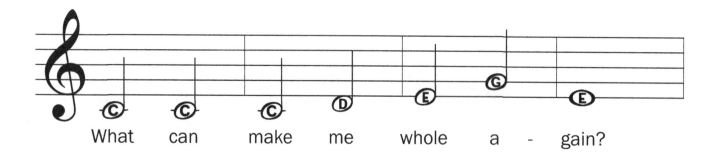

What can make me whole a - gain?

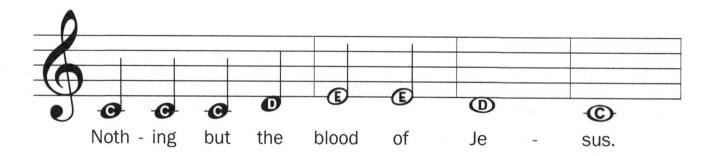

Noth - ing but the blood of Je - sus.

Nothing but the Blood of Jesus

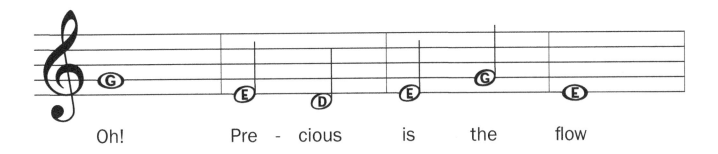

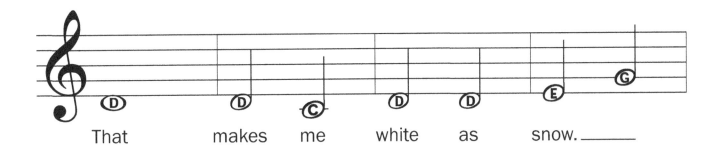

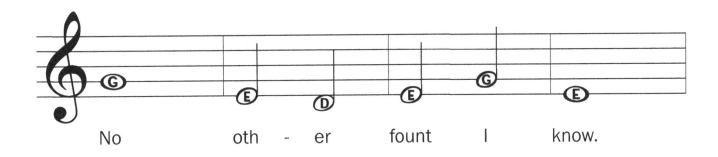

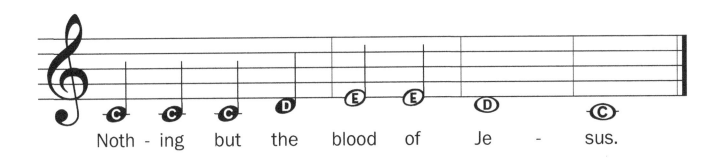

Oh, How I Love Jesus

Frederick Whitfield

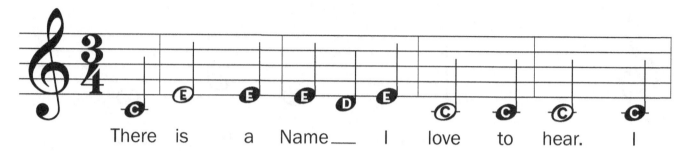

There is a Name___ I love to hear. I

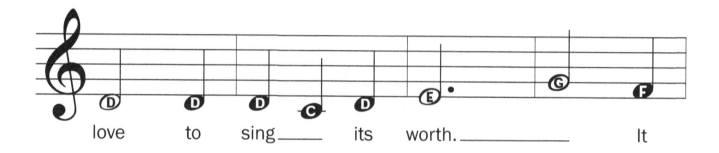

love to sing___ its worth._____ It

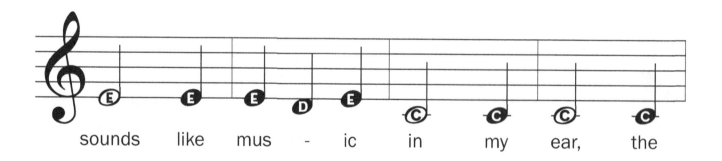

sounds like mus - ic in my ear, the

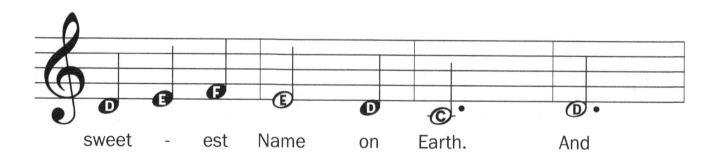

sweet - est Name on Earth. And

Oh, How I Love Jesus

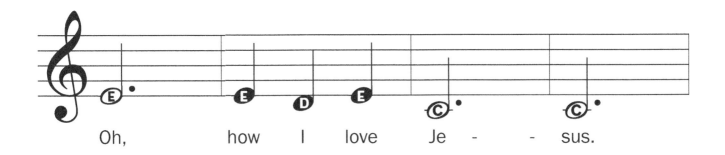

Oh, how I love Je - - sus.

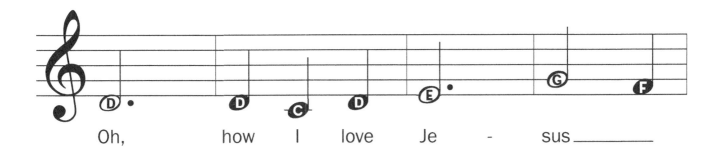

Oh, how I love Je - sus____

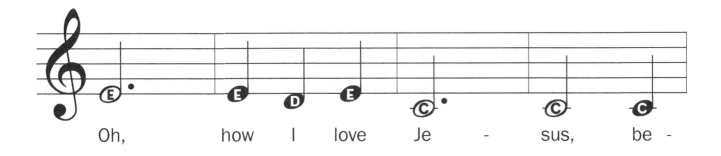

Oh, how I love Je - sus, be -

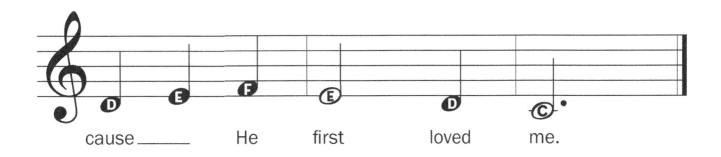

cause____ He first loved me.

Level Two

The songs in Level Two add two notes.

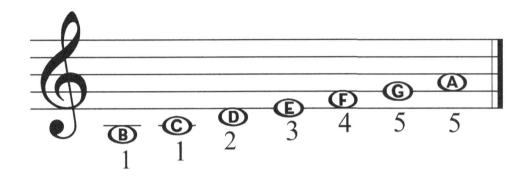

Move fingers one and five to the side to reach the new notes.

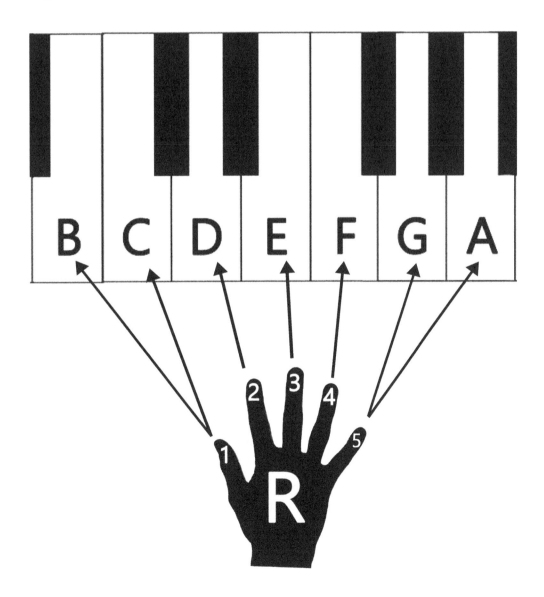

Michael, Row the Boat Ashore

African American Spiritual

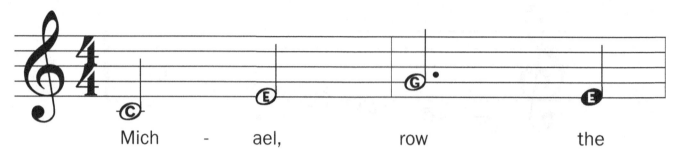

Mich - ael, row the

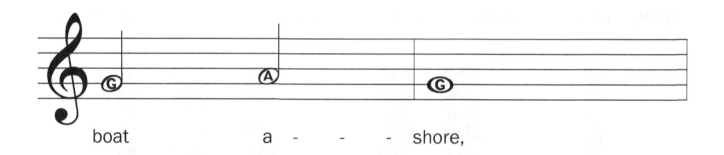

boat a - - - shore,

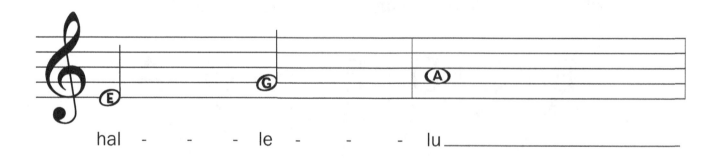

hal - - - le - - - lu_____

_____ jah!

24

Michael, Row the Boat Ashore

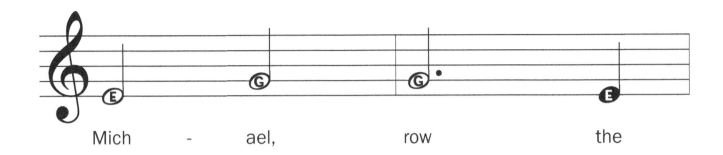

Mich - ael, row the

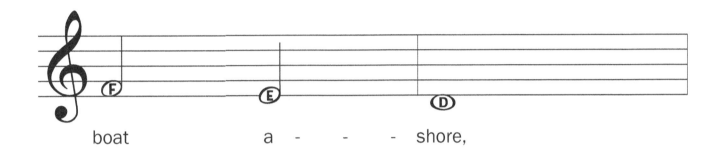

boat a - - - shore,

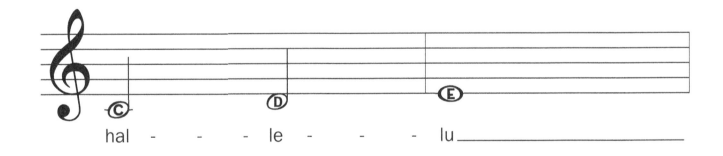

hal - - - le - - - lu_____

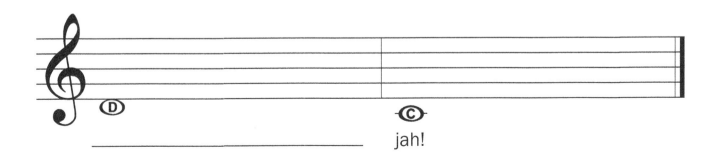

_____ jah!

When I Survey the Wondrous Cross

Isaac Watts and Lowell Mason

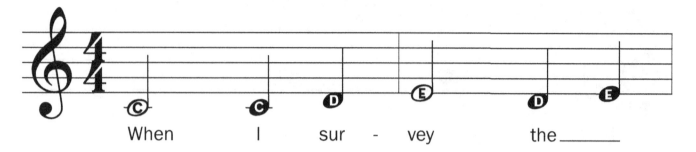

When   I   sur - vey   the _____

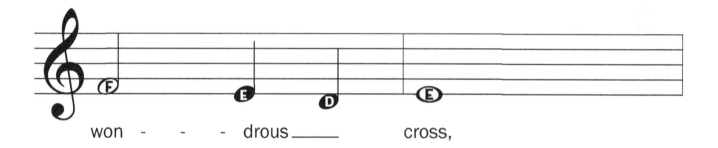

won - - - drous _____   cross,

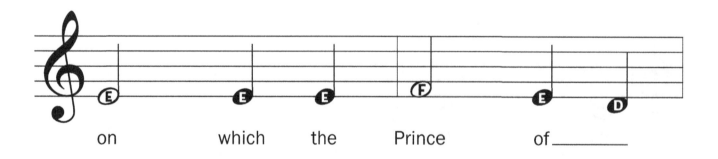

on   which   the   Prince   of _____

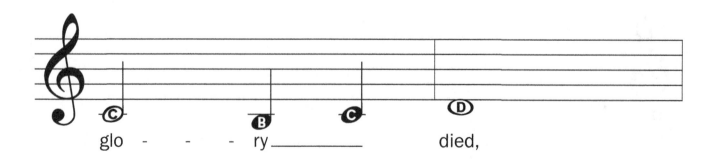

glo - - - ry _____   died,

When I Survey the Wondrous Cross

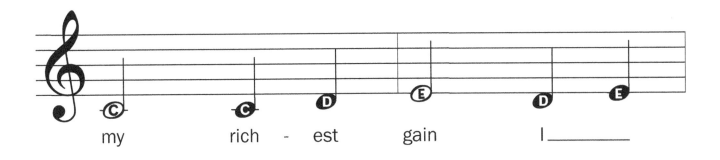

my   rich - est   gain   I _____

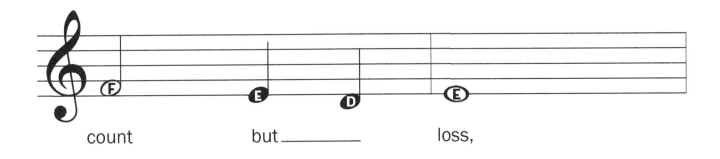

count   but _____   loss,

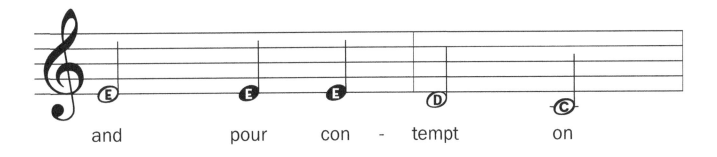

and   pour   con - tempt   on

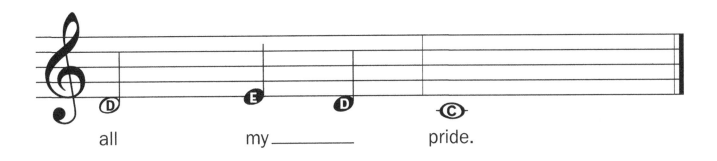

all   my _____   pride.

Abide with Me

Henry F. Lyte and William H. Monk

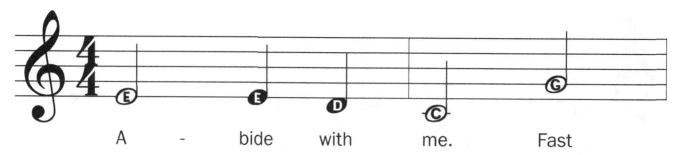

A - bide with me. Fast

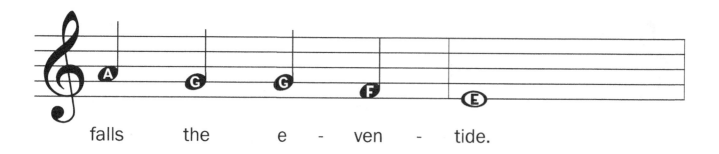

falls the e - ven - tide.

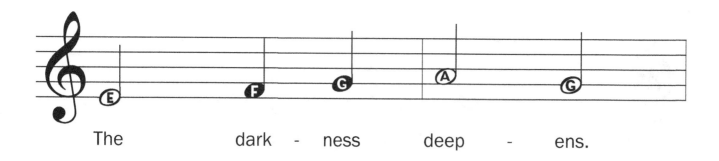

The dark - ness deep - ens.

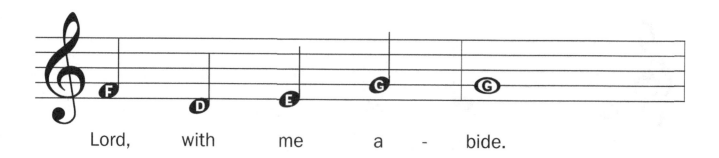

Lord, with me a - bide.

Abide with Me

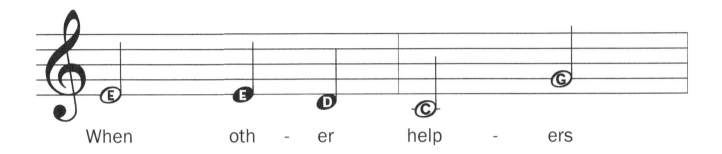

When   oth - er   help - ers

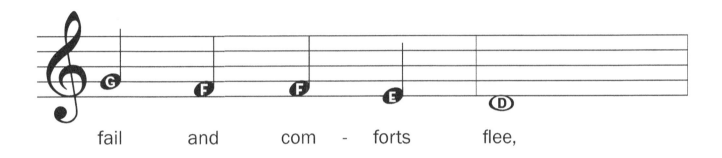

fail   and   com - forts   flee,

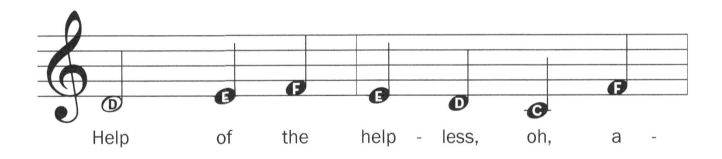

Help   of   the   help - less,   oh,   a -

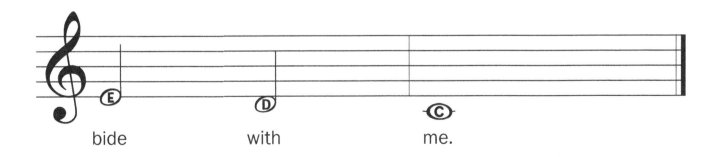

bide   with   me.

He's Got the Whole World in His Hands

African American Spiritual

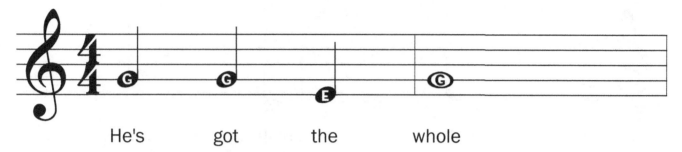

He's   got   the   whole

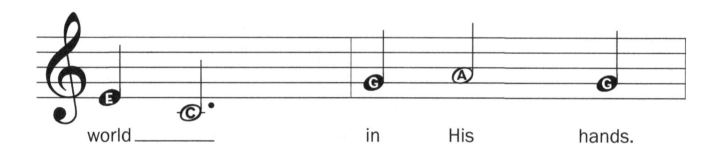

world _____   in   His   hands.

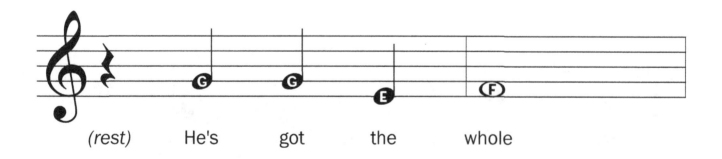

(rest)   He's   got   the   whole

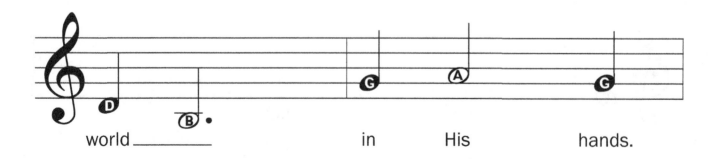

world _____   in   His   hands.

He's Got the Whole World in His Hands

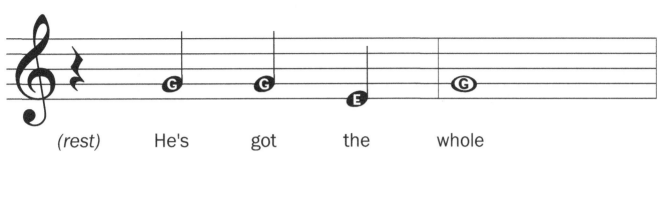

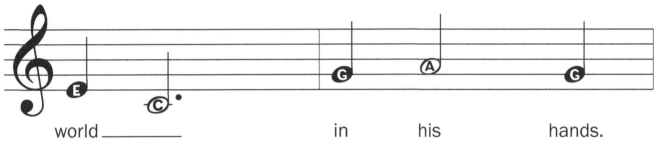

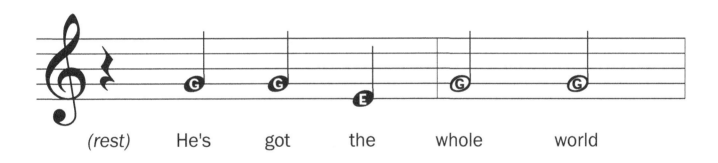

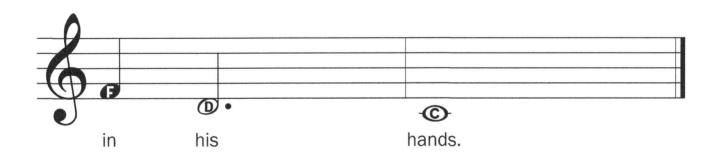

Do Lord

African American Spiritual

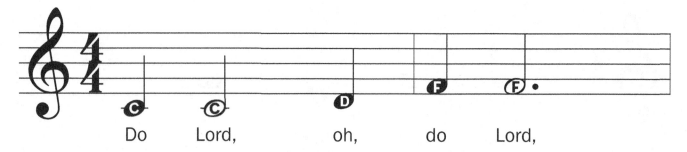

Do   Lord,   oh,   do   Lord,

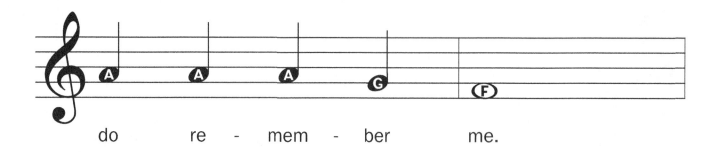

do   re -   mem -   ber   me.

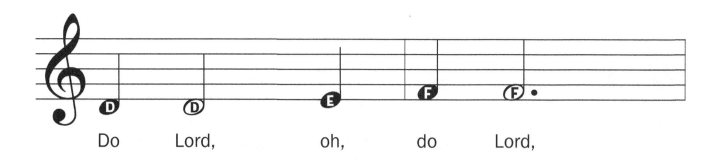

Do   Lord,   oh,   do   Lord,

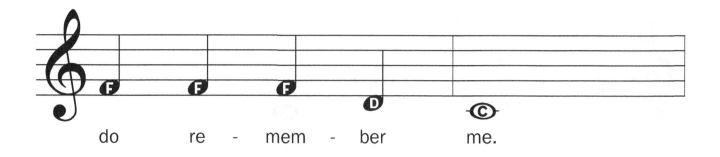

do   re -   mem -   ber   me.

Do Lord

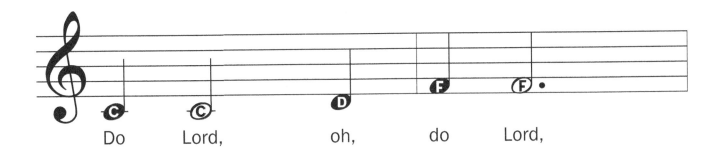

Do   Lord,   oh,   do   Lord,

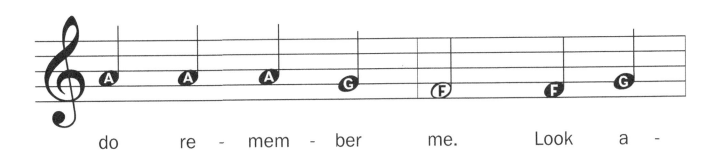

do   re - mem - ber   me.   Look   a -

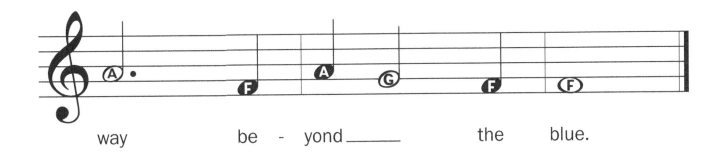

way   be - yond_____ the   blue.

Turn Your Eyes Upon Jesus

Helen Howarth Lemmel

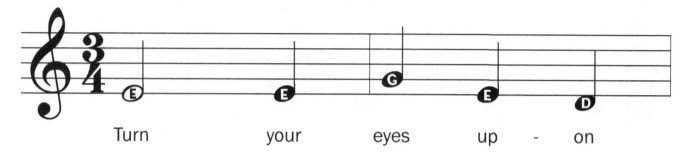

Turn   your   eyes   up - on

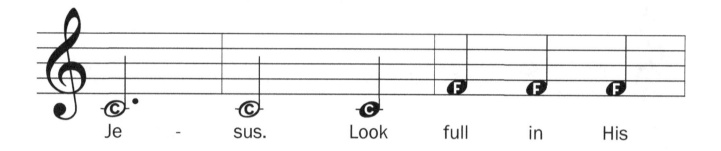

Je - sus.   Look   full   in   His

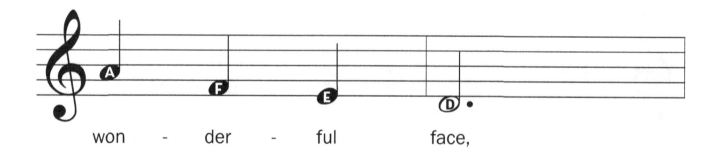

won - der - ful   face,

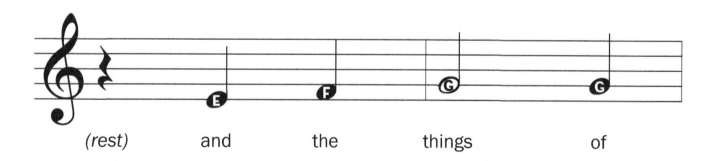

(rest)   and   the   things   of

Turn Your Eyes Upon Jesus

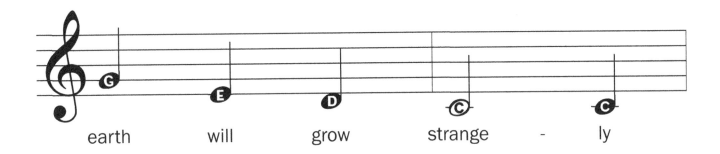

earth   will   grow   strange - ly

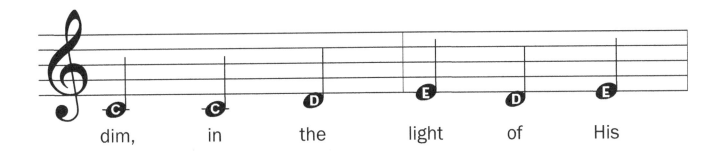

dim,   in   the   light   of   His

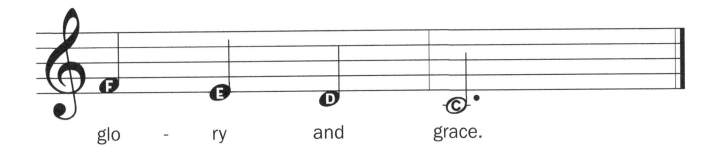

glo - ry   and   grace.

Come, Thou Fount of Every Blessing

Robert Robinson and John Wyeth

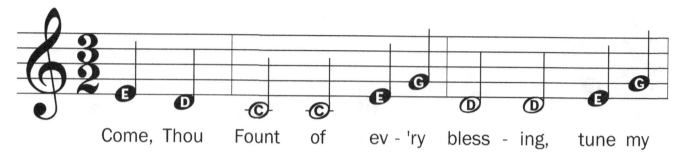

Come, Thou Fount of ev - 'ry bless - ing, tune my

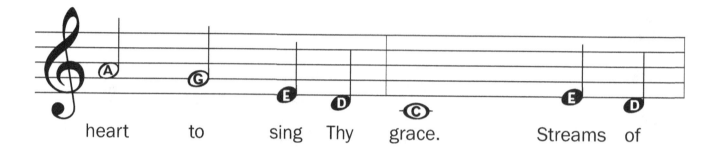

heart to sing Thy grace. Streams of

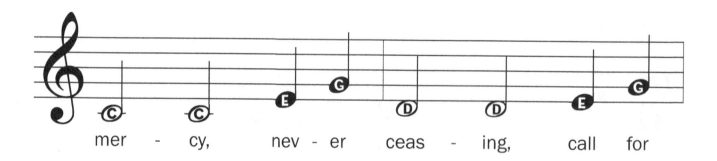

mer - cy, nev - er ceas - ing, call for

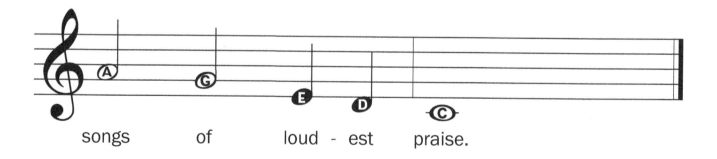

songs of loud - est praise.

Nearer, My God, to Thee

Sarah Flower Adams and Lowell Mason

Near - er, my God, to Thee,

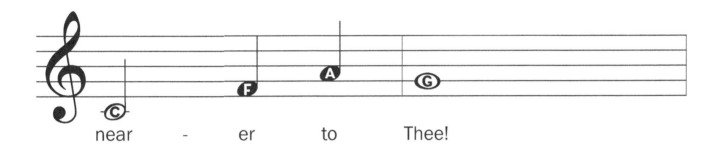

near - er to Thee!

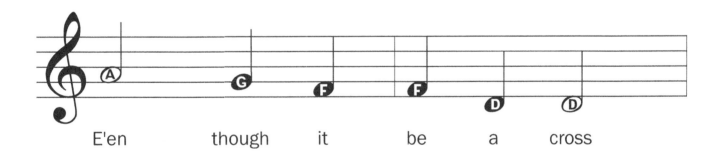

E'en though it be a cross

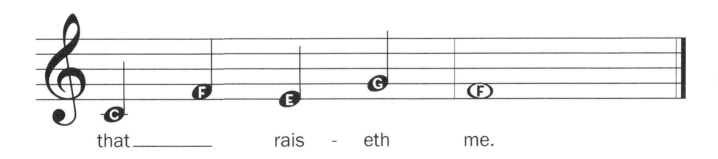

that_____ rais - eth me.

I've Got Peace Like a River

African American Spiritual

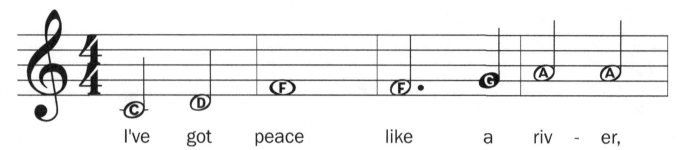

I've got peace like a riv - er,

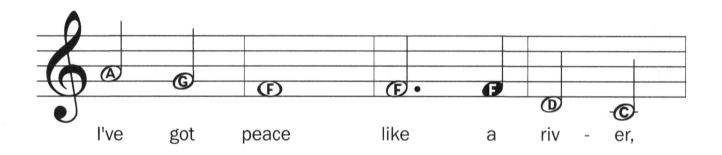

I've got peace like a riv - er,

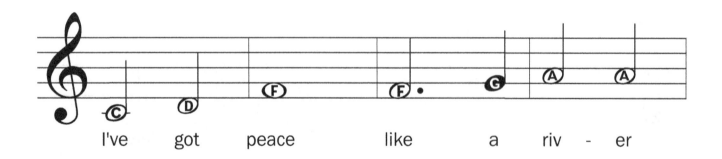

I've got peace like a riv - er

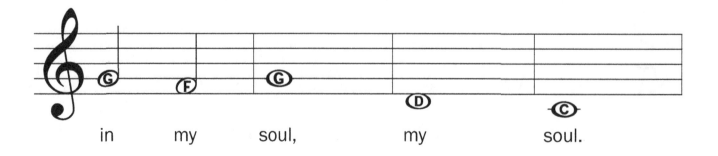

in my soul, my soul.

I've Got Peace Like a River

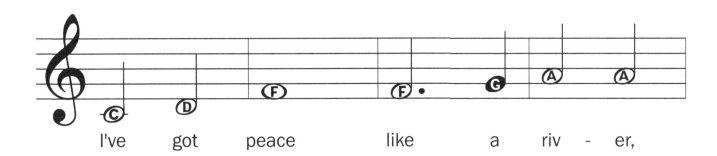

I've   got   peace   like   a   riv - er,

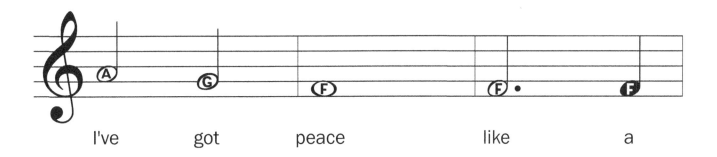

I've   got   peace   like   a

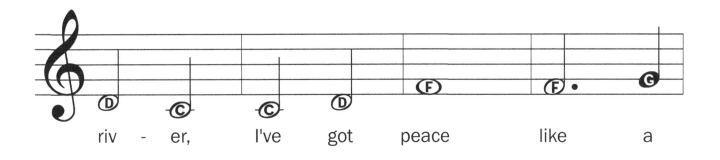

riv - er,   I've   got   peace   like   a

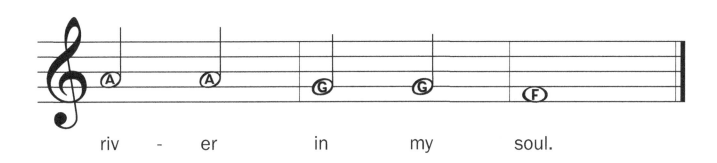

riv - er   in   my   soul.

At the Cross

Isaac Watts and Ralph Erskine Hudson

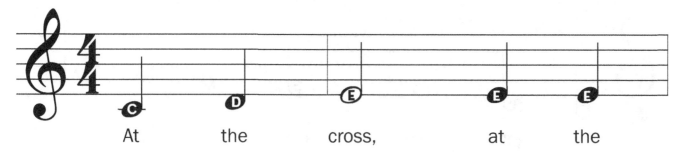

At   the   cross,   at   the

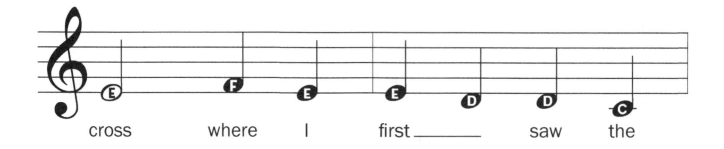

cross   where   I   first _____ saw   the

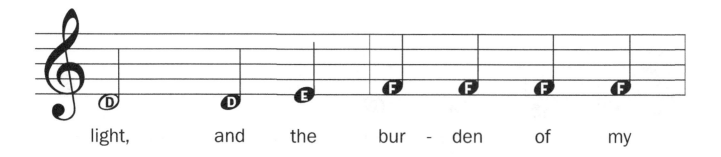

light,   and   the   bur - den   of   my

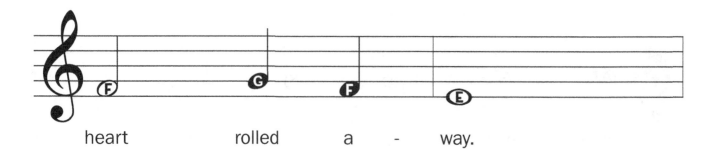

heart   rolled   a - way.

At the Cross

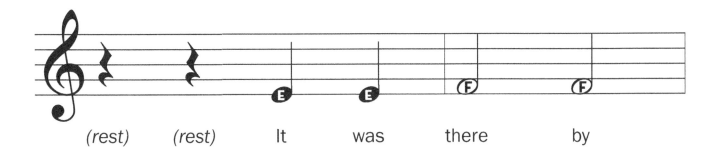

(rest)   (rest)   It   was   there   by

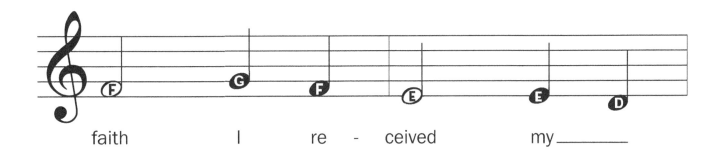

faith   I   re - ceived   my_____

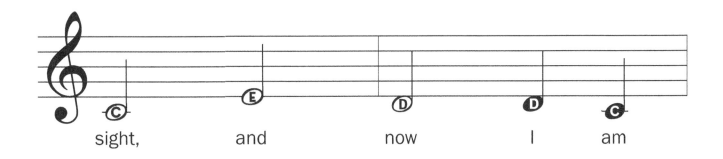

sight,   and   now   I   am

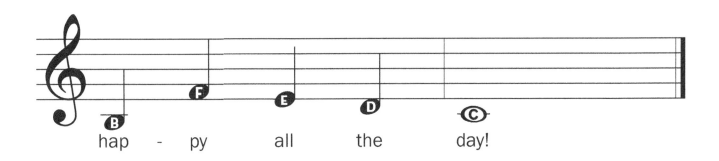

hap - py   all   the   day!

Trust and Obey

John H. Sammis and Daniel B. Towner

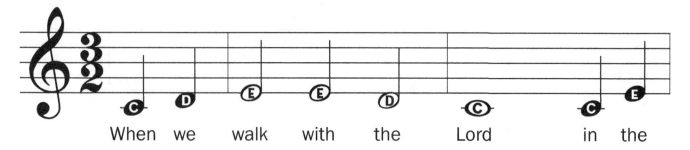

When we walk with the Lord in the

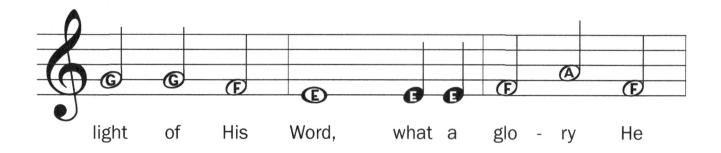

light of His Word, what a glo - ry He

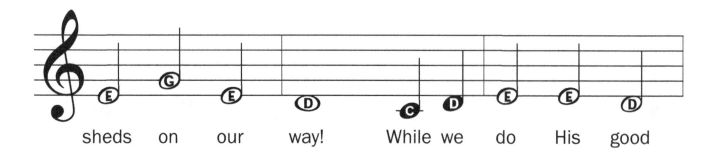

sheds on our way! While we do His good

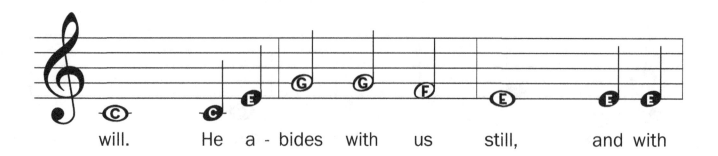

will. He a - bides with us still, and with

Trust and Obey

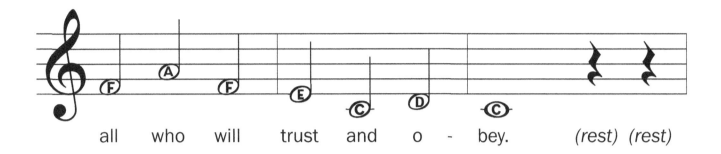

all who will trust and o - bey. *(rest) (rest)*

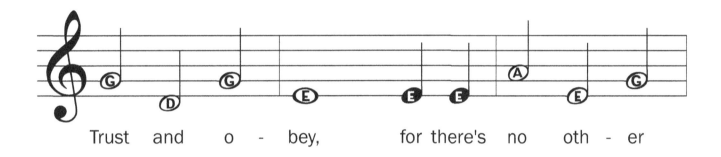

Trust and o - bey, for there's no oth - er

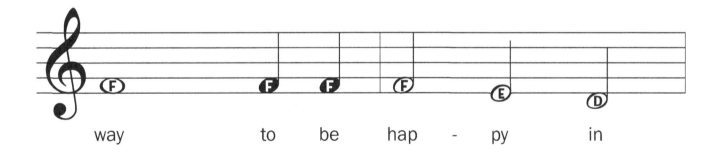

way to be hap - py in

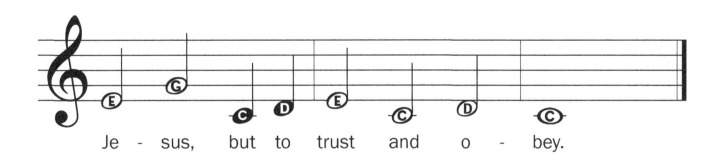

Je - sus, but to trust and o - bey.

Glory to His Name

E.A. Hoffman and John H. Stockton

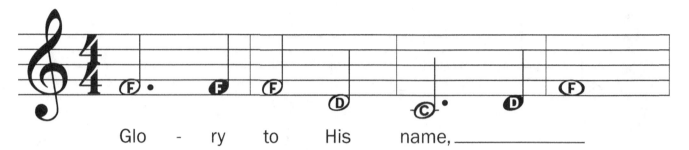

Glo - ry to His name, _____

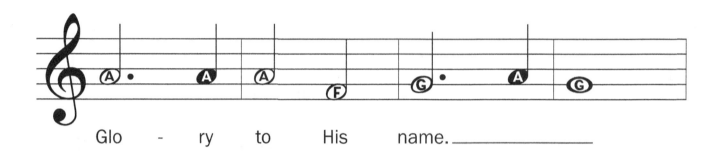

Glo - ry to His name. _____

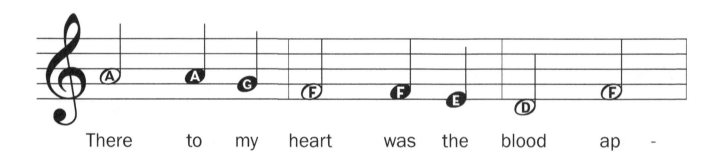

There to my heart was the blood ap -

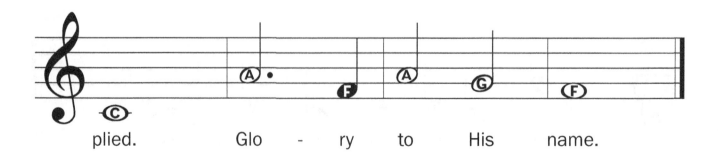

plied. Glo - ry to His name.

Alas, and Did My Savior Bleed

Isaac Watts

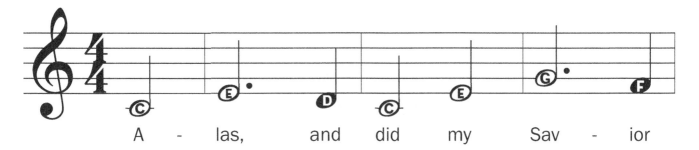

A - las, and did my Sav - ior

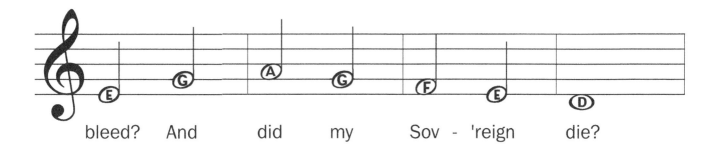

bleed? And did my Sov - 'reign die?

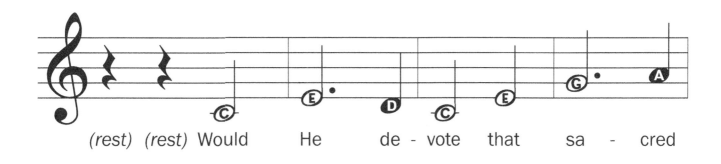

(rest) (rest) Would He de - vote that sa - cred

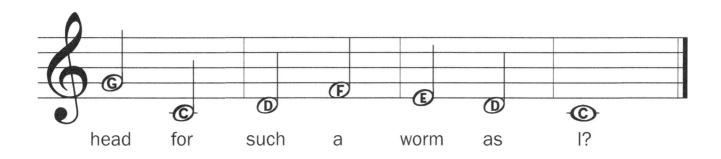

head for such a worm as I?

This Little Light of Mine

African American Spiritual

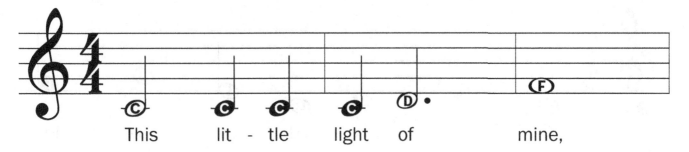

This   lit - tle   light   of   mine,

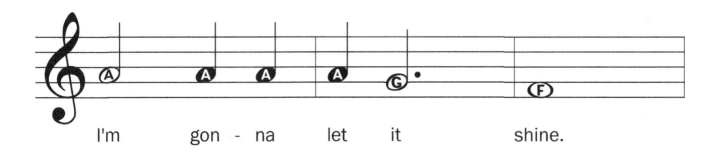

I'm   gon - na   let   it   shine.

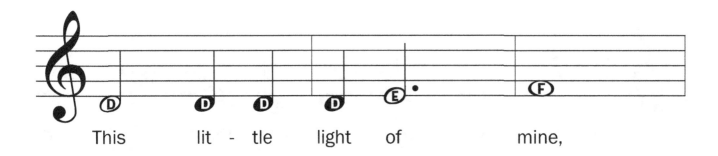

This   lit - tle   light   of   mine,

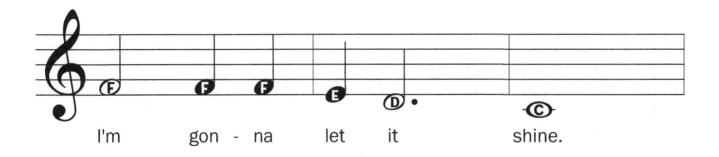

I'm   gon - na   let   it   shine.

This Little Light of Mine

Level Three

The songs in Level Three use both hands.

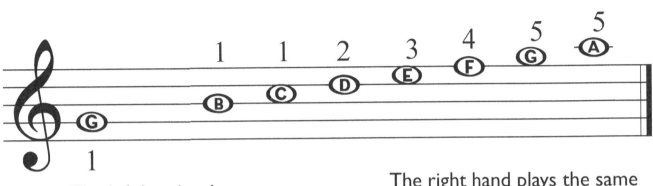

The left hand only plays one note.

The right hand plays the same notes, but sits higher to make room for the left hand.

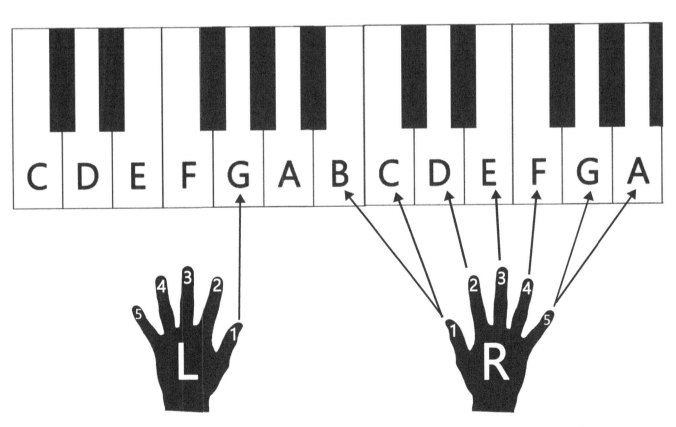

Find the G closest to the right hand and place your left thumb on it.

Take My Life and Let It Be

Frances R. Havergal

Take My Life and Let It Be

All Hail the Power of Jesus' Name

Edward Perronet and Oliver Holden

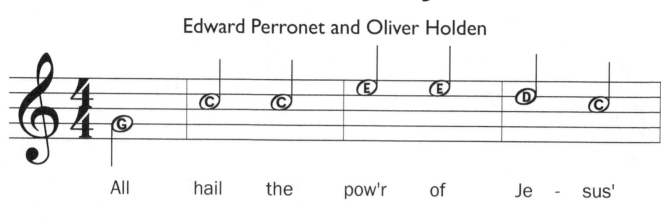

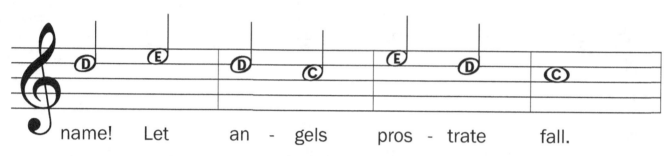

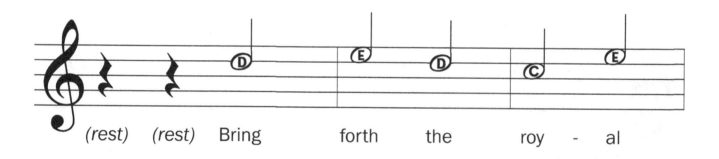

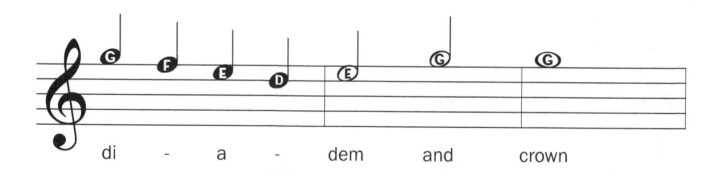

All Hail the Power of Jesus' Name

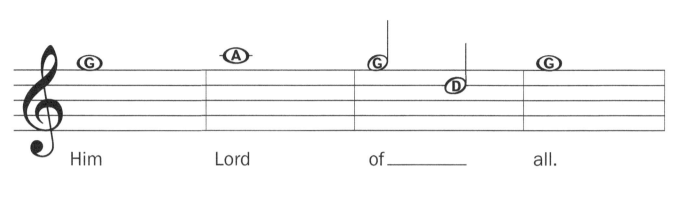

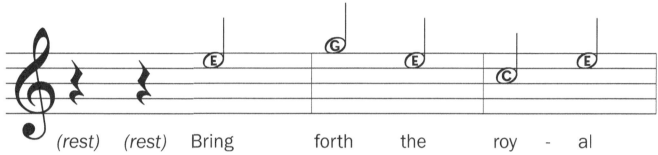

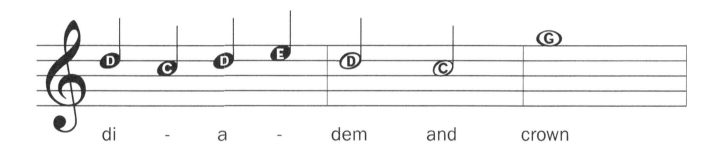

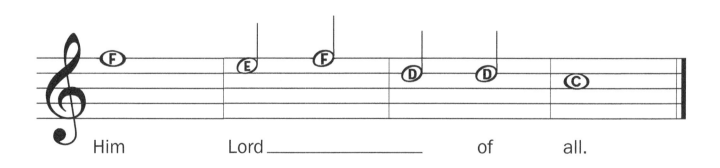

My Jesus, I Love Thee

William R. Featherstone and Adoniram J. Gordon

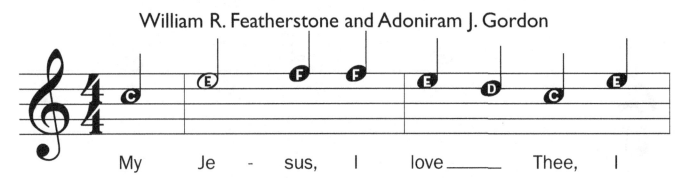

My   Je - sus,   I   love _____ Thee,   I

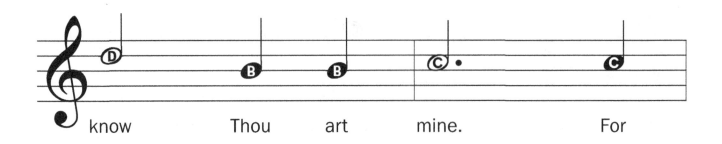

know   Thou   art   mine.   For

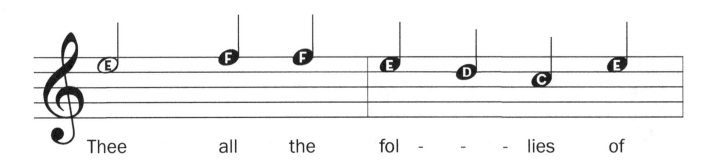

Thee   all   the   fol - - - lies   of

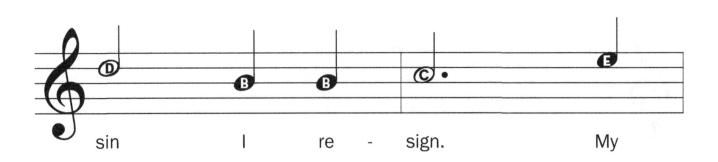

sin   I   re - sign.   My

My Jesus, I Love Thee

Come, Thou Almighty King

Anonymous and Felice de Giardini

Come, Thou Almighty King

Blest Be the Tie That Binds

John Fawcett and Hans Georg Nägeli

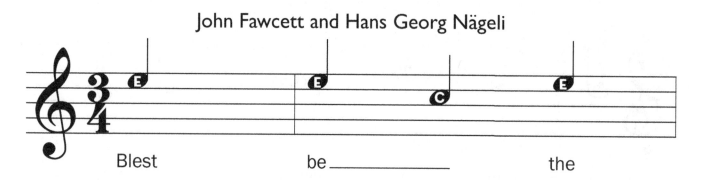

Blest   be _____   the

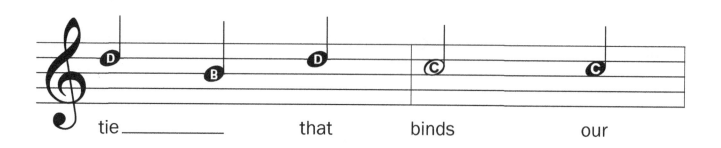

tie _____   that   binds   our

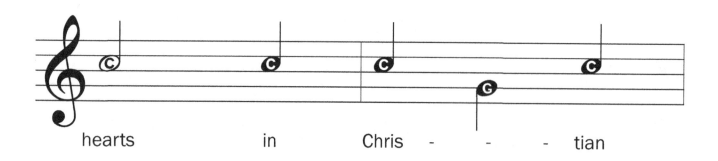

hearts   in   Chris   -   -   - tian

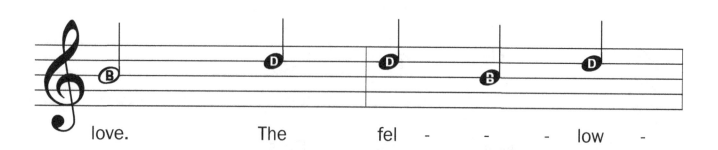

love.   The   fel   -   -   - low   -

Blest Be the Tie That Binds

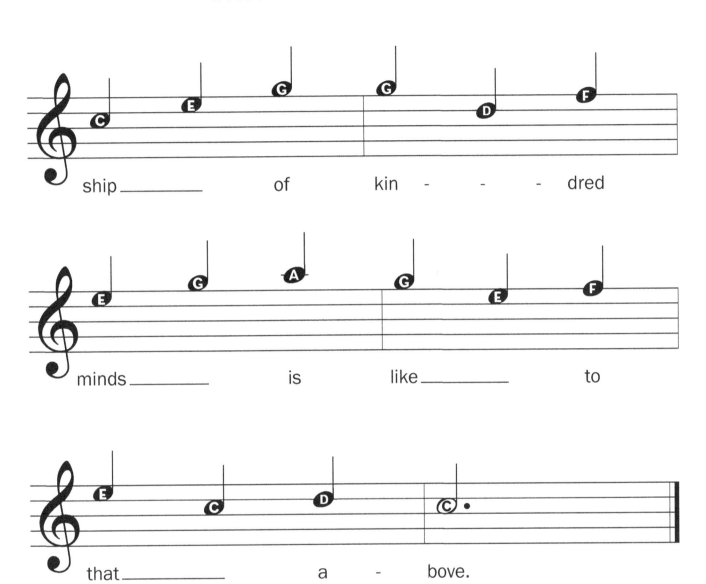

Level Four

The songs in Level Four use three left hand notes.

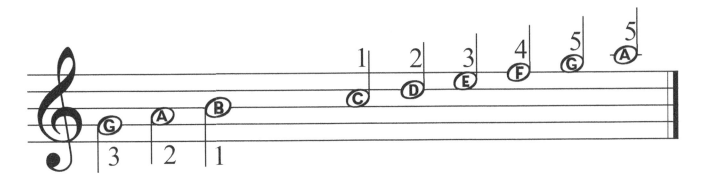

The left hand plays notes with the stem pointing down.

The right hand plays notes with the stem pointing up.

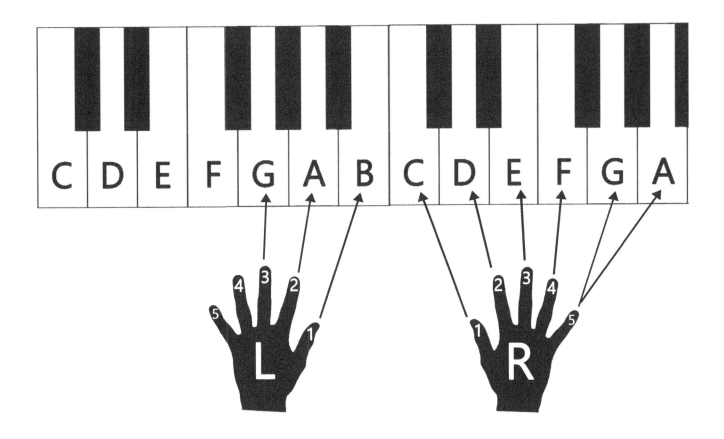

Your thumbs will sit beside each other on the keyboard.

For notes without a stem, use the notes around them as a guide, or check this chart to see which hand should play the note.

Doxology

Thomas Ken and Louis Bourgeois

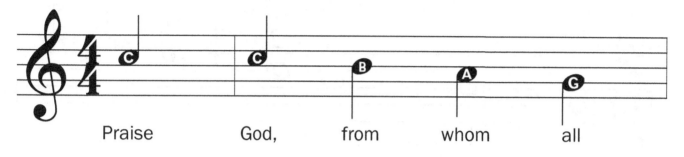

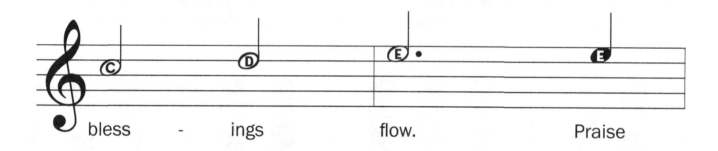

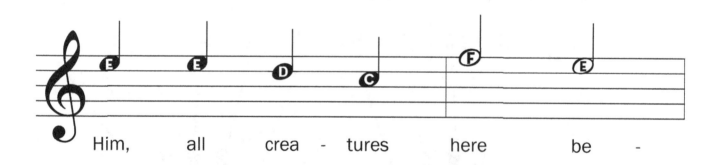

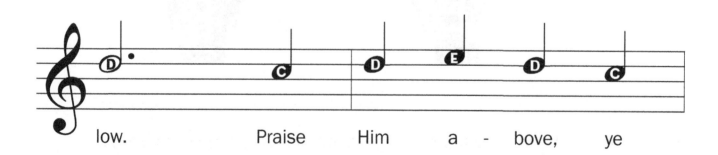

Doxology

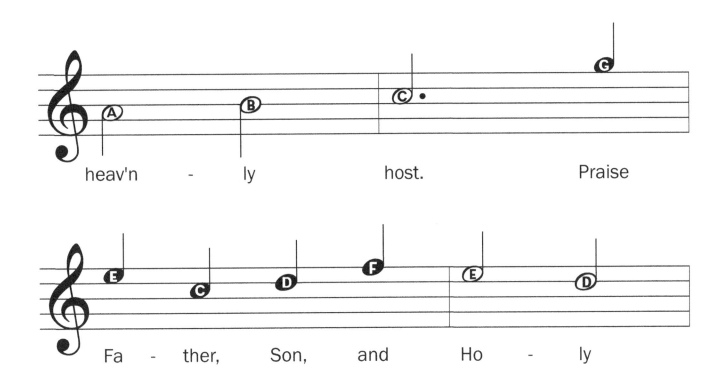

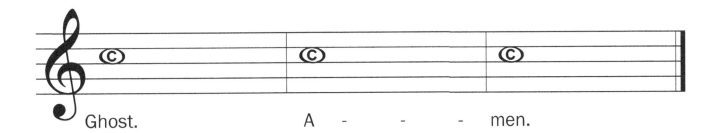

Amazing Grace

John Newton and E. O. Excell

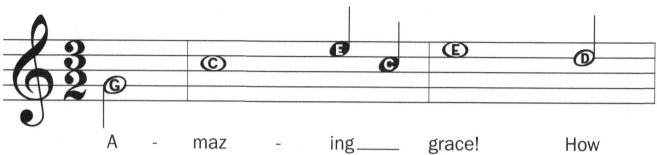

A - maz - ing____ grace! How

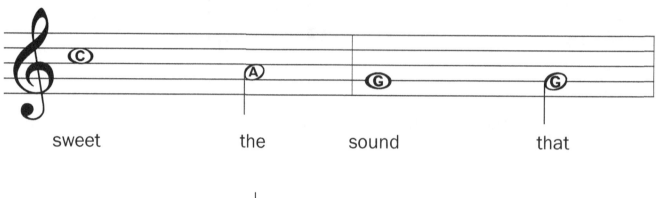

sweet   the   sound   that

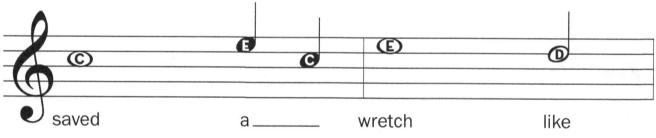

saved   a____   wretch   like

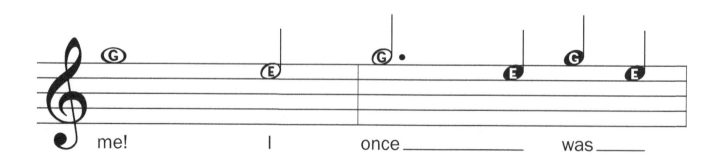

me!   I   once____   was____

Amazing Grace

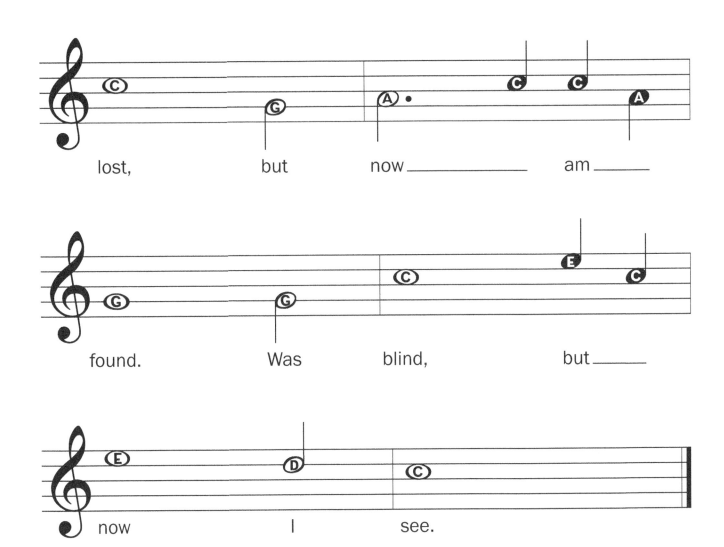

Are You Washed in the Blood?

E. A. Hoffman

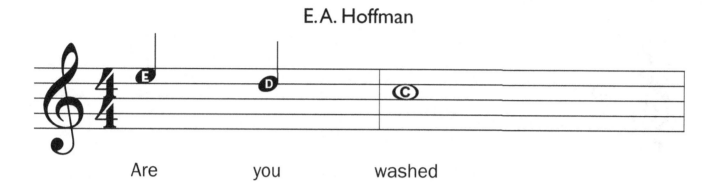

Are   you   washed

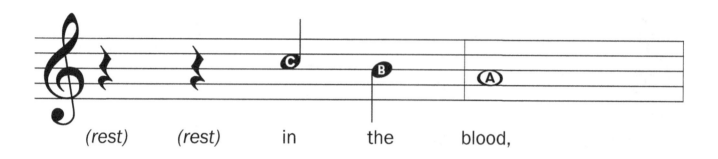

(rest)   (rest)   in   the   blood,

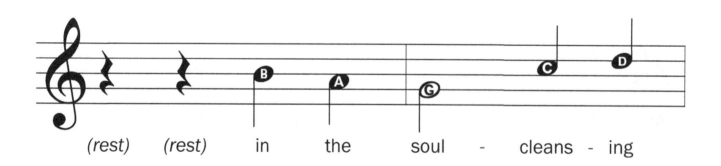

(rest)   (rest)   in   the   soul - cleans - ing

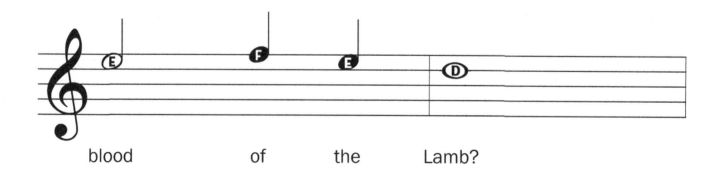

blood   of   the   Lamb?

Are You Washed in the Blood?

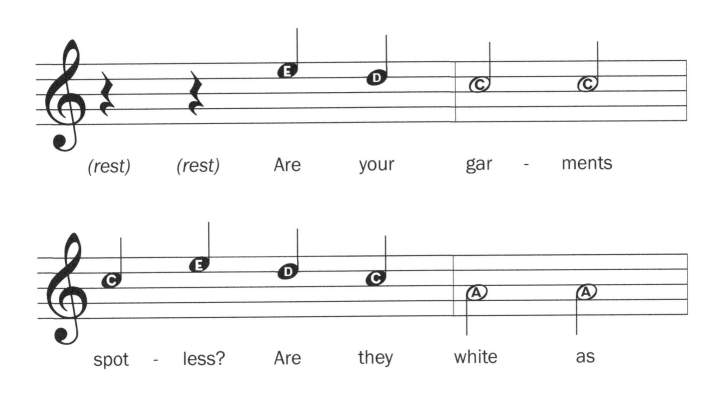

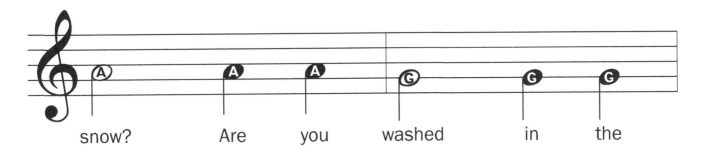

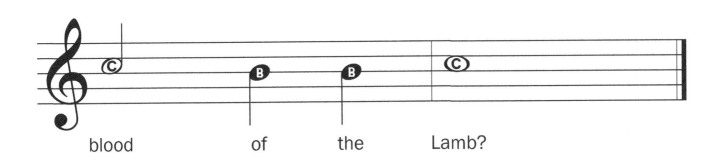

Rock of Ages, Cleft for Me

Augustus M. Toplady and Thomas Hastings

Rock of Ages, Cleft for Me

flowed,   be   of   sin   the   dou - ble

cure.   Cleanse me   from   its guilt and pow'r.

For the Beauty of the Earth

Folliott Sandford Pierpoint and Conrad Kocher

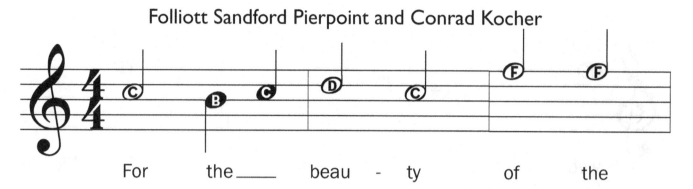

For the beau - ty of the

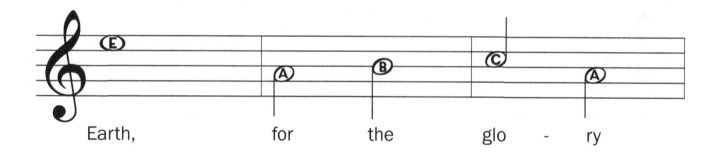

Earth, for the glo - ry

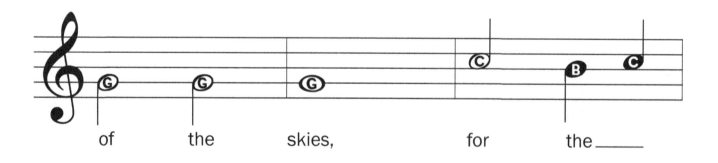

of the skies, for the

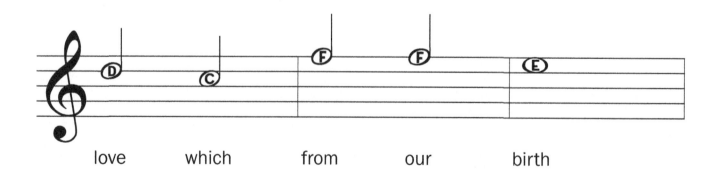

love which from our birth

For the Beauty of the Earth

I Need Thee Every Hour

Annie S. Hawks and Robert Lowry

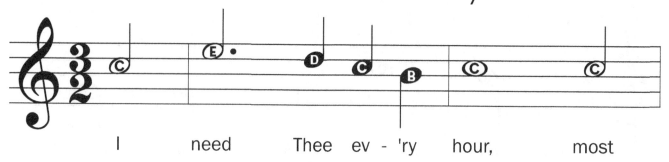

I   need   Thee   ev - 'ry   hour,   most

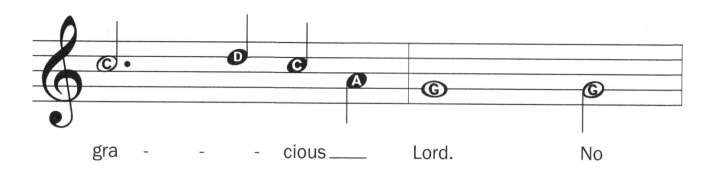

gra - - - cious___   Lord.   No

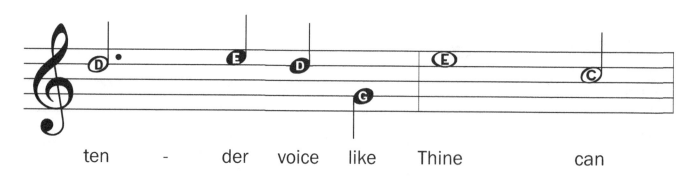

ten - der   voice   like   Thine   can

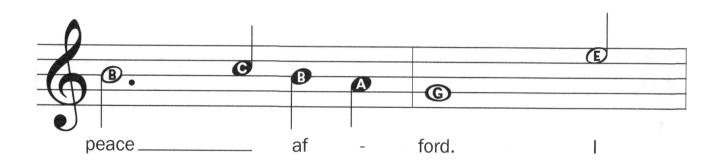

peace_____ af - ford.   I

I Need Thee Every Hour

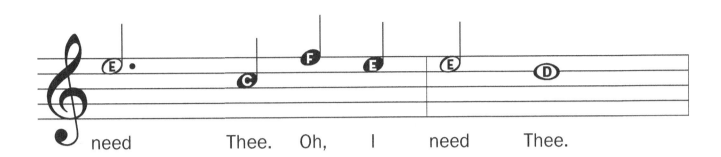

need   Thee.   Oh,   I   need   Thee.

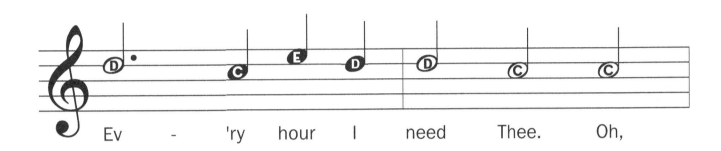

Ev - 'ry   hour   I   need   Thee.   Oh,

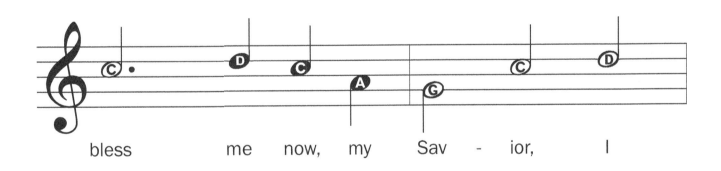

bless   me   now,   my   Sav - ior,   I

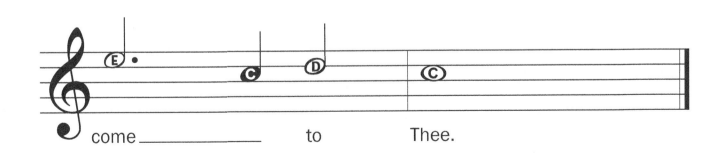

come_____   to   Thee.

Jesus, Keep Me Near the Cross

Fanny Crosby

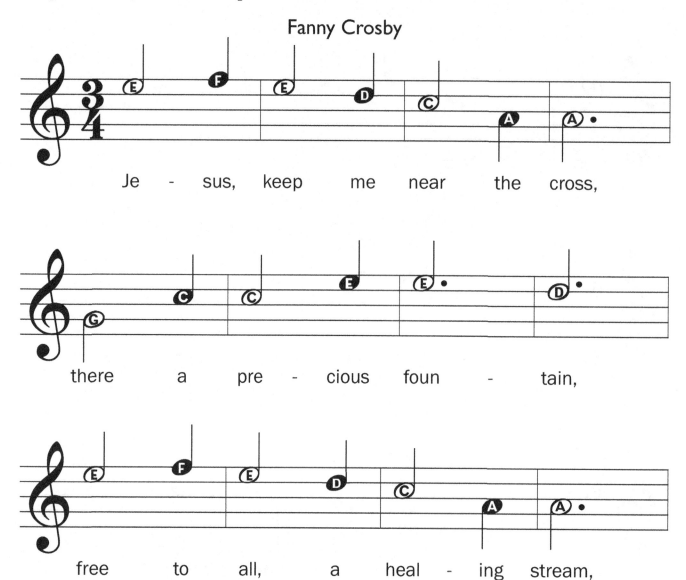

Je - sus, keep me near the cross,

there a pre - cious foun - tain,

free to all, a heal - ing stream,

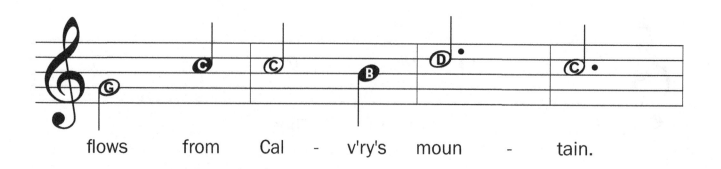

flows from Cal - v'ry's moun - tain.

Jesus, Keep Me Near the Cross

Leaning on the Everlasting Arms

E. A. Hoffman and A. J. Showalter

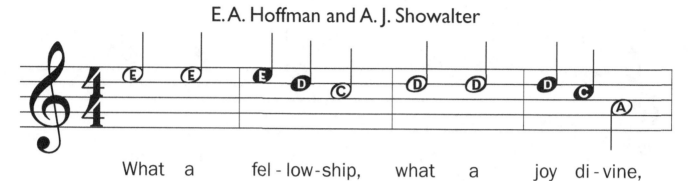

What a fel-low-ship, what a joy di-vine,

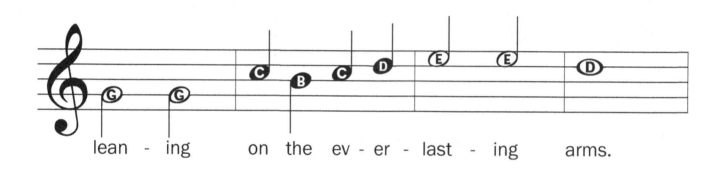

lean - ing on the ev- er - last - ing arms.

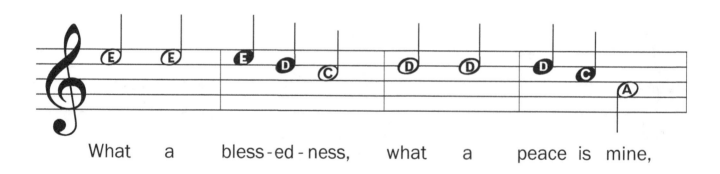

What a bless-ed-ness, what a peace is mine,

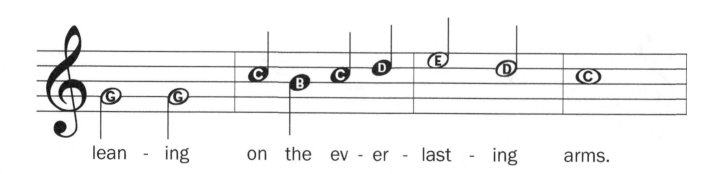

lean - ing on the ev- er - last - ing arms.

Leaning on the Everlasting Arms

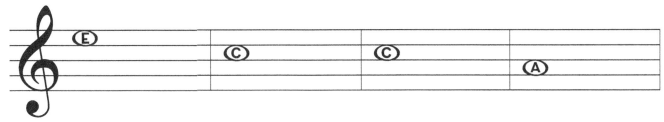

Lean - - ing,   lean - - ing,

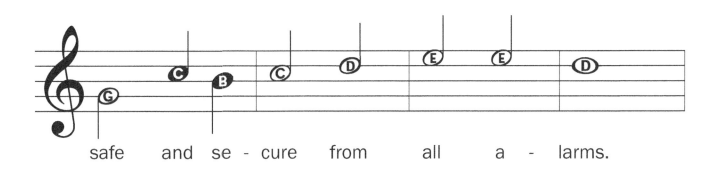

safe   and   se - cure   from   all   a - larms.

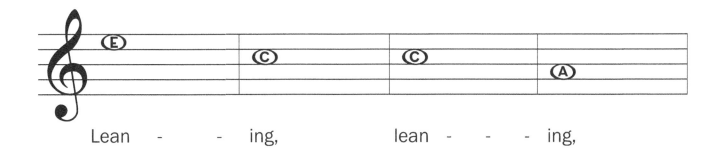

Lean - - ing,   lean - - ing,

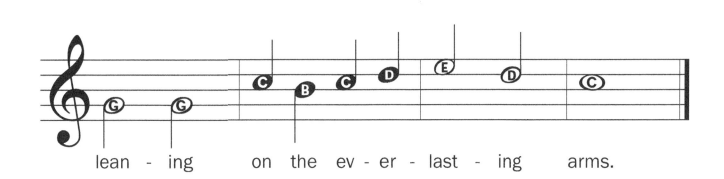

lean - ing   on   the   ev - er - last - ing   arms.

Simple Gifts

Joseph Brackett

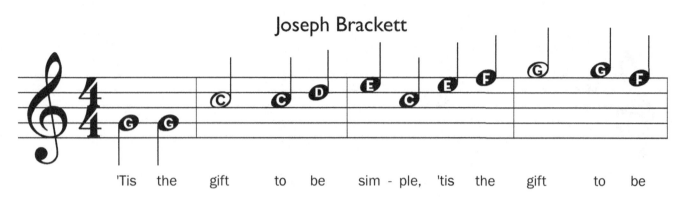

'Tis the gift to be sim - ple, 'tis the gift to be

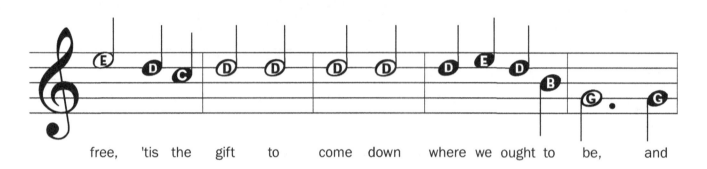

free, 'tis the gift to come down where we ought to be, and

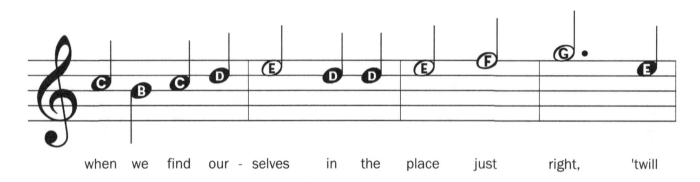

when we find our - selves in the place just right, 'twill

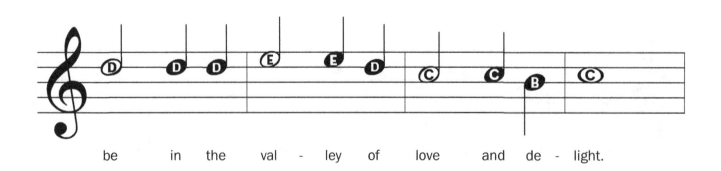

be in the val - ley of love and de - light.

Simple Gifts

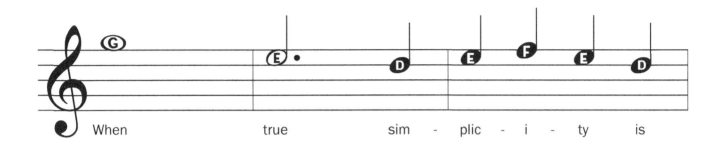

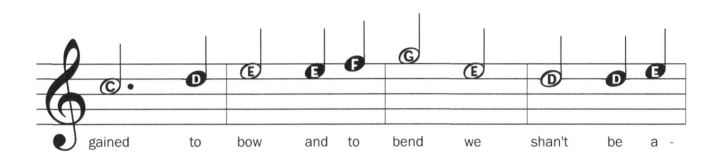

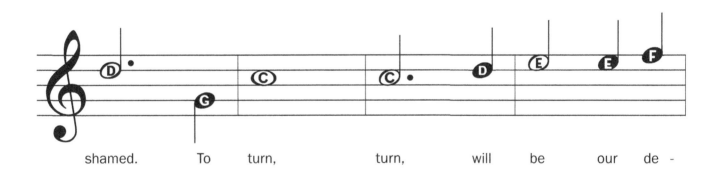

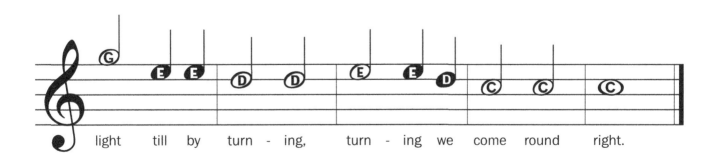

79

To God Be the Glory

Fanny Crosby

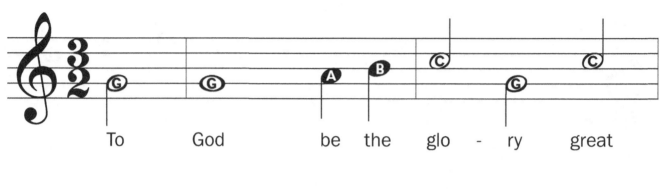

To God be the glo - ry great

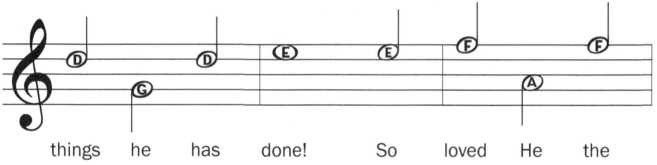

things he has done! So loved He the

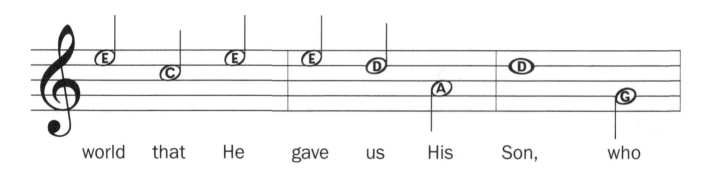

world that He gave us His Son, who

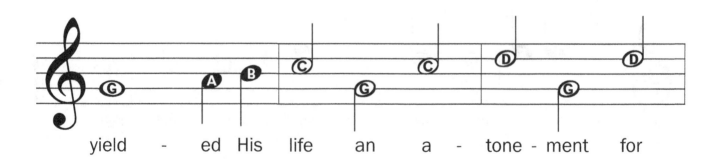

yield - ed His life an a - tone - ment for

To God Be the Glory

sin   and   o - pened   the   life - gate   that

all   may   go   in.   Praise   the

Lord!   Praise   the   Lord!   Let   the

Earth   hear   His   voice!   Praise   the

Song continues on next page ⟶

To God Be the Glory (continued)

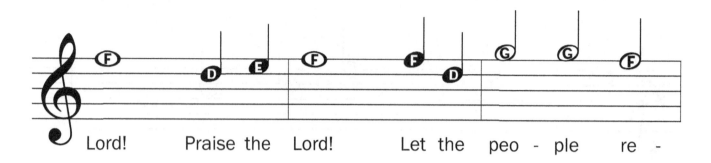

Lord! Praise the Lord! Let the peo - ple re -

joice! Oh come to the Fa - ther, through

Je - sus the Son, and give Him the

glo - ry! Great things He has done.

Oh for a Thousand Tongues to Sing

Charles Wesley, Carl G. Gläser, and Lowell Mason

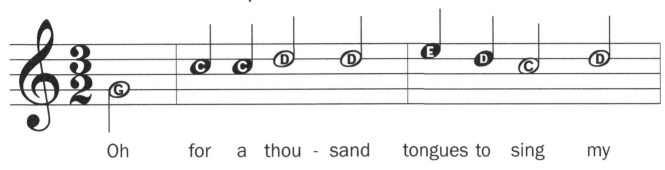

Oh for a thou - sand tongues to sing my

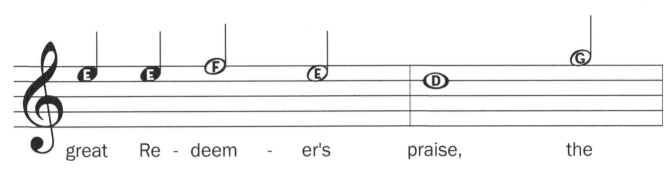

great Re - deem - er's praise, the

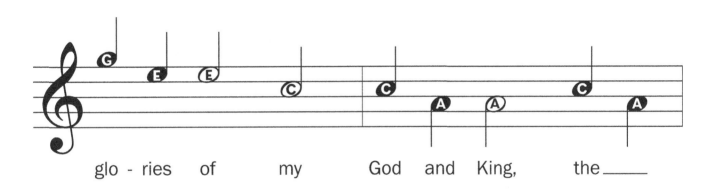

glo - ries of my God and King, the ___

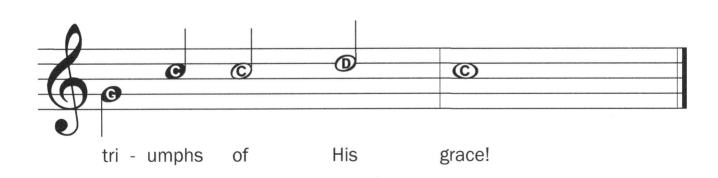

tri - umphs of His grace!

Bonus Downloads

This book includes free digital content.
Visit **www.avanellpublishing.com** or scan the QR code below
to access your bonus materials,

- Fully orchestrated recordings of each song

- Printable reference charts to use while you play

- Lessons and charts for left hand playing

- Practice tips to help you build your skills

- Sheet music of additional songs

Made in the USA
Las Vegas, NV
16 September 2023

77684310R00050